Calming Mandala

Coloring Book

Butterfly Edition

Illustrator - Joseph Rabie
Publisher - Evard Publishing

www.calmingmandala.com
www.evardpublishing.com

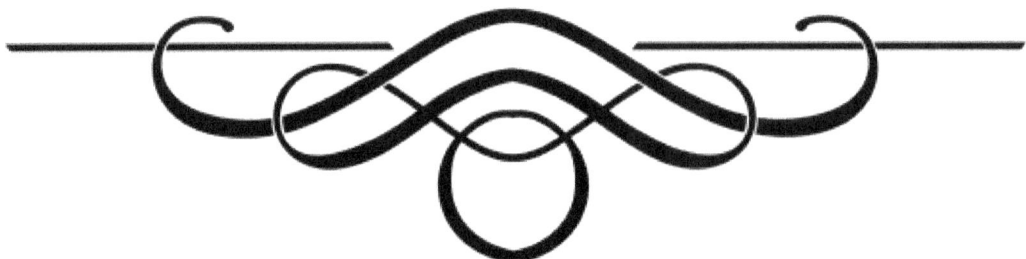

This Book Belongs to:

....

www.ingramcontent.com/pod-product-compliance
Lightning Source LLC
Chambersburg PA
CBHW081659270326
41933CB00017B/3218